By Abraham Great
Copyright ©2013 Revised 2020
ISBN: 978-1-908040-27-5

Published in the UK by:
Golden Pen Publishing Ltd

Golden Pen (Publishing)
A Division of Golden Pen LTD
Milton Keynes,
United Kingdom

info@goldenpenpublishing.com
www.goldenpenpublishing.com

Cover design by Media Expression Intl (Check this)
Printed in the UK

DEDICATION

I have been been a committed lover of the word of God from the age of 16. Just by reading the bible, I have found courage, strength, wisdom, understanding, power, joy, blessing, and family. However, the one thing I know the Bible continues to help me make is decisions. So, I would like to dedicate this book to the WORD.

APPRECIATION

I moved into top gear in obedience to God's word and my mentors' instructions since 2004. This feat I owe to one person: my wife, Queen Great. Not only have you been a great companion in making the right decisions, but you have also been meek enough to make a right turn after realizing every wrong decision made. For the motivation to write this book while raising wonderful children- a great inspiration to us both- with me, I say thank you!

To my son, Abraham Darren Great, to you, I owe the title of this book and the inspiration to write it. Thank you for the listening ears during those telephone conversations in the car, which eventually culminated in the idea behind this book. A leader you are, and that you will always be. To Dexter and Divine, thank you for being on your wisest behaviors each time daddy is busy teaching or writing. You guys are Great.

This book would not have been available for print without the help of volunteers at Gr8terworks, Bola Adebola, Maxwell, Eniola Olajide, Victoria Agunbiade, and Ketochi Ekpo. You guys are a great blessing and joy.

To my Big Bro, Gbenga Oladokun, A.K.A Concept, you have consistently delivered amazing results despite the deadlines and hard work your daily routine requires, thank you ever so much.

To all HLBC members, I thank you for the privilege of serving as your leader, teaching these principles that work. Indeed, it is working.

Finally, to my editor, Olusegun Iseilaiye, your ability to interpret my intentions is incredible. Thank you for your help, inspiration, and patience through this project. You are destined for the top. To Dr. Boye Oloritun, thank you for spending several hours to proofread this work. You are blessed in many ways.

INTRODUCTION

From the inception of time, the responsibility of being the primary decision-maker has rested on the shoulders of a man. One of the first assignments given to Adam in Genesis was to DECIDE which name God's other creations will be called. Upon this foundation is man's leadership position established - from the family level. And this universal status quo is here to stay, regardless of mounting modern ideologies.

The ability to make sound decisions is one of the true tests of manhood. It is a key component of leadership. The decisions you make as a man shapes people's perception of you and informs their decision on whether or not to follow your lead. You would recall the event of the fall of man in the Bible. Why would God question only Adam even though it was Eve who first took the forbidden fruit and shared with him afterward? Well, he was supposed to be the key decision-maker, being the one God gave the instruction, but allowed Eve to decide for him. God expected him to take charge and not fall for whims or dance to the beats of others- in this case, the serpent and Eve, his wife.

Going further, history has walked us through different times when kingdoms have risen, empires have been extended, and uprisings have led to revolutions - mostly by the decisions of male figures- from Xerxes to Caesar; from Che Guevara to Sankara, just to name a few. Today, things have not changed. Even without being a national figure, the fate of the home continues to be attributed to the man of the house. He takes credit first before anyone else for a successful family and takes the most blame for failure. When the community experiences insecurity, it is the men who decide to form vigilante groups to protect the neighborhood. So, you see, the ability to make decisions and act on them is crucial to the existence of man. It is the key determinant of his worth and impact.

This is the backdrop that informs the decision to write this book- to help every man make decisions that will make him valuable so that he may continue to succeed and be relevant to his world. The instructions in this book, if faithfully and diligently followed, will set you on a pedestal that you will not fail at being your best. Amazing results abound for you all ramifications, so much that you will become a reference point, an exact life example when the occasion to define a man of real value arises. By meeting the requirements stated herein, your credibility and reliability as a man will never be questioned. It will cause your life to take a drastic positive turn, in case you have missed in so many ways.

There is really no congenitally extraordinary man, only those who have had extraordinary lives, occasioned by the right decisions that have injected an abundance of values into them. And out of this abundance, they are sharing out to affect their world positively. You are only one read away from joining this league of men. Launch, therefore, into the chapters and walk on to that glorious ground, where your footprint will forever be indelible.

31

DECISIONS
THAT MAKES
A MAN OF
VALUE

Life begins with decisions

Abraham Great

CONTENT

DECISION TO WORK

1. DECISION TO WORK

"From the fruit of their lips people are filled with good things, and the work of their hands brings them reward." - Proverbs 12:14 (NIVUK)

Everything God made has a purpose to serve. Man is not an exception. The first thing God gave man after creating him and planting him in Eden was work- to dress and take care of the garden. This is where the foundation of the male folk's primary purpose was laid. Though the specialty may differ, one common denominator basic to the definition of every true man on the face of the earth is his WORK. It is therefore unthinkable for any man to be satisfied with being idle. One of the most common questions in people's curious mind about any man they know nothing about is what he does for a living, or where he works. As a man, your work is a basic credential that constitutes your identity.

WHY WORK?

There is a whole lot of noteworthy reasons to work, few of which are giving below:

➤ IT GETS YOU PAID

Whosoever does not work, let him not eat. So says the Bible. Only those who have something doing are entitled to get paid. You can demand any amount you think you deserve and the one who hires you can afford to pay- whether an employer or a client. But for someone who does not work, he has no prerogative to dictate how much to be given. A beggar has no choice.

➤ IT PREVENTS IDLENESS

When a man has nothing doing, he is wasting his time. And a waste of time is a waste of life. Our life is a summation of our time. No wonder it is called a lifetime. The best way to be of no significance is to be idle. Work keeps us engaged and presents us with an opportunity to add value to people and institutions which you get financial rewards for. While doing that, you are also adding value to yourself.

➤ IT ELEVATES MAN

Work is what sets us on the path of progress in life. Being diligent and productive increases the value people place on us and brings us recognition. A man diligent in his endeavor will stand will attract the attention of highly placed people. The Bible confirms this.

➤ IT DIGNIFIES MAN

Regardless of what you do or how much you get, once you have something doing, people in their right mind will automatically treat you with respect. This is because you are not at anyone's mercy and you are seen as responsible. How do you take responsibilities in your immediate and extended family if you do not work? And how would you expect to be treated with honour when you shoulder no responsibility?

WHAT TO CONSIDER BEFORE YOU DECIDE TO WORK

When you want to decide what to do, first you must ensure it is not one within the boundaries set by the law. The dignity that comes with labour is priceless. So, you don't want to trade your pride and reputation in a bid to get wealth. Also, it is gross indiscretion to put yourself on the wrong side of the law in the quest for survival. A good name the Bible says is better is more desirable than great wealth.

You should also consider the morality of your job. This is because a job may be legitimate in the eyes of the law, but not right in the eyes of God. You should not go into the business of marijuana, prostitution, or pornography just because it is legitimate in the country, state, or region you reside in. Such engagements and many other ones are destructive to lives and sinful in God's eyes, despite the legitimacy it may have gained in some regions of the world.

Lastly, you should what you really love and enjoy doing. The money your work fetches you is not on a par with the joy and fulfillment you derive from doing what you love. If you sign up for something you detest, especially when you have an option, you are doing yourself a disservice as you may never find joy doing it, no matter how much you are being paid. Whenever challenges come to question your competence, you will have a hard time getting by. The whole world will seem to be on your shoulder. What is supposed to be an adventure-filled endeavour will seem like a nightmare. But if you are on a job that activates your joy, every challenge comes as an opportunity to explore and get better at what you know how to do best. When your work gives you fulfillment, it is a sign that you are fitting into your purpose.

HOW DO YOU APPROACH WORK?

It is not just enough to decide to work, you must possess the right attitude. Many employees feel weary and bitter about their work because of their demands. So, you hear them say it is not easy. But hey, it is work. It is not supposed to be easy. It is not fun. Some are of the opinion that as employees, they are pursuing the goals of other people. But you need to start viewing the work as yours. Think of the success of every assignment and the profile you are building by that means. That way you can start to view your work as a way to achieve your goals too. You think they are using you, but everybody needs somebody to achieve their own goals. Even if you are the CEO, think of the service your company renders, then you would realize that it is helping your client achieve their goal, and that way, your company is also achieving its goal. No matter what you do or whom you work for, start seeing yourself as your biggest project. And this project is worth the best of investment. Even if you work for hire, view it as a step to your dream. Make a self-development plan. Set goals for your life and career. The pursuit of these goals takes hard work. And sometimes it takes working for hire too. Bear in mind that you also learn while you earn.

But if you honestly do feel like your work does not align with your goals, maybe it is time to change your career to one in which your passion lies. You may come to a point where all work may seem mind-numbing to you. But in the mean-time, while seeking an opportunity to explore your passion, either by seeking another paid job or venturing on your own, give your best to whatever you are doing at the moment, no matter how tough. That resilience-building up in you will come handy when finally venture into your passion, especially when it not yet bringing you the desired returns.

"Once you start a working on something, don't be afraid of failure and don't abandon it. People who work sincerely are the happiest."

Chanakya

"It is the working man who is the happy man. It is the idle man who is the miserable man."

Benjamin Franklin

DECISION TO THINK

2. DECISION TO THINK

"It is a trap to dedicate something rashly and only later to consider one's vows." - Proverbs 20:25

Thinking is an integral part of the nature of every living being- man and animals. We all process mentally the things we see, hear, feel, and do. This means the things we do and the way we conduct ourselves are a reflection of our thoughts. The outcome of our enterprises shows the quality of thoughts we have given to it. Some people think their way into success, while others think it into much trouble. So, making a decision to think, and think right is a non-negotiable ingredient of a well-lived life.

Though thinking is a natural ability, it is subject to training. We must train our minds to engage in productive thinking. Everything we see around is a product of thoughts. The skyscrapers, airplane, Internet, and any other thing you can think of. The world as we have it today is a result of a combination of different thoughts.

Being a positive thinker is a decision, though it is more challenging as you have to go against the stream. You need to make conscious efforts to become a positive thinker. Productive thinking is positive thinking. A positive thinker tries to reason out solutions and identify opportunities in the midst of challenges. Being a productive thinker may also require thinking out of the box.

Out-of-the-box thinking is also positive thinking. It is what births novel ideas as it involves defying rules and crossing boundaries of the norm in the mental realm

A negative thinker on the other hand focuses on the problem, the bad news, the possibility is things getting worse.

Even when all is well, a negative thinker sees the bad in every good. Negative thinking is destructive thinking and you must deliberately decide against it.

That thinking is natural does not mean that it happens effortlessly. Thinking is hard work. It requires time and effort. The act of dedicating time and effort to thinking is what brings about profound solutions to challenges. This is how innovations are birthed.

There are deep thinkers and there are shallow ones. Which one would you rather be? The decision to be mentally diligent is what differentiates these two with results to show.

"I like thinking big. If you're going to be thinking anything, you might as well think big."

Donald Trump

"Thinking is the hardest work there is, which is probably the reason why so few engage in it."

Henry Ford

DECISION
TO ACT

3. DECISION TO ACT

"Multitudes, multitudes, in the valley of decision! For the day of the Lord is near in the valley of decision." - Joel 3:14.

Every decision starts with a thought and ends with an action. Until you act-the DOING PART- your decision-making process is not complete. It is what breathes life to whatever you have decided. Action is what makes your resolve come to fruition.

While deciding to act is good, you must recognize that not every action produces results. The timing of your action is crucial to its outcome. Your action must be timely. This means you must be proactive.

Crises are normal in every sphere of life. When they come, the approach you take in managing them will determine how things turn out. It either gets resolved when well managed or spirals out of control if poorly handled. SO, you would do well to analyze your remedial measures. However, the remedial measure is not as powerful as preventive tactics. Proactiveness is the only way to prevent crises. Instead of having to explain to your customers how you sent damaged goods to them, is it not better to have envisaged every factor that would tamper with the process of production and delivery and prevented them? To be proactive, you must take a long look ahead for every unfavourable possibility, and a wide look around for internal and external factors that won't play right for your business. Sitting down and waiting for a problem to happen before you start to find a solution is a lazy approach to life; you should have imagined the problem ahead of time. You may ask, 'how about unforeseen circumstances?', but I tell you that most of them are aftermaths of oversights. As much as you can, always keep an ear to the ground to prevent being caught unawares.

Being proactive applies to every other aspect of life. In your career, you must keep analyzing to figure out the future. Based on current trends and dynamics, are your skills going to remain relevant in the coming years or you will be replaced by machines? Ask yourself hard questions and be brutally honest about the answers you get. With these, you will be able to chart the next course of action and begin to take practical steps so that your decisions can bear fruits. A secure future is one that is adequately and rightly prepared for today. The time to act is now.

Have you just started a business? Do not wait for the clients to come to you or call you. Make the phone calls, follow up with emails, and bait the hook.

It is important to understand that you need to start forming new useful habits once you've made the decision to become proactive. Some of us may have a real struggle in this area of life, due to the wrong passive habits formed in us by our family or school. You cannot hope to 'eat this elephant' all at once. You need to break it down into pieces and eat each piece one by one. The big decision to become proactive won't do you much good unless you come up with smaller and practical decisions.

How about your family life? Be sensitive. Figure out the needs of your family members even before they express it. Forgive first and do not wait for your loved ones to come to you and ask for forgiveness. Being proactive within the family circle means you are responsible and loving. And love is reciprocal. It becomes easy to make a sacrifice when situations demand. Then the bond becomes stronger. Show your love first and do not wait for others to show love to you.

Yes, becoming proactive demands a high level of courage and careful attention to details. You need to be a brave person to start acting first. It brings amazing dividends. Making the first step can do wonders in your life. Just imagine how many opportunities you might have missed staying passive!

So, make up your mind and decide to be active. Then make a list of small things you can change and small proactive habits you can introduce into your life. Start acting upon your list and never give up.

"Give the best you have, and it will never be enough. Give your best anyway."

Mother Theresa

"In the final analysis, it is between you and God. It was never between you and them anyway."

Mother Theresa

DECISION TO COMMUNICATE

4. DECISION TO COMMUNICATE

"Now then, my sons, listen to me; pay attention to what I say." - Proverbs 7:24

Communication involves four main activities, each of which we all must be skilled in, in order to be effective. They are: speaking, listening, writing, and reading. We encode messages by speaking or writing, while we decode by listening or reading. Let us take a brief look at them in groups of two:

SPEAKING AND WRITING: When communicating our thoughts, feelings, and opinions to others either by speaking or writing it, one thing we must do is be clear. Whomever we are communicating with is not in our mind. Do not speak implicitly, holding back on full expression under the assumption that the other party has a clue. If you detest a particular thing, for example, let the other party know that you are not pleased and give salient reasons. Be detailed enough. Sometimes you accuse people of not listening when actually, you are not fully expressive. Half information sometimes is as good as misinformation. This failure in communication is the cause of so many needless conflicts in relationships. And when caution is not taken, it heads south till it eventually crash-lands.

LISTENING AND READING

Listening and reading areas key communication skills that every human being should possess. Sadly, many people take no cognizance of their importance. Whenever you hear people talk about failure to communicate, check it; at the root of the matter is one or both parties talking, but failing to listen to (or read attentively) the other. This has led many businesses, professional and personal relationships down a sour path. It never has to be this way. Listening and reading cost nothing, yet the reward is priceless. You just need to get over your lack of patience.

If you have functioning (or well aided) ears and eyes, then you are capable of listening and reading excellently. Though it goes beyond merely subjecting your ears to hearing the sound of the other person's words and your eyes to reading the text. There is such a thing as reading between the lines. There are things to consider in developing a good listening skill and explained below:

> WE ARE ALL DIFFERENT

One of the worst things to do while communicating is to assume that your audience sees the world the same way you do. We all are different. We reason differently. Even when listening to the same words, we process according to our level of comprehension, and orientation. We come from different backgrounds where different words mean different things. This has to be taken into consideration as you learn to communicate properly. You must be as clear as you can possibly be.

> KEEP THE BALANCE

There is something that seems to be a formula of universal balance - 20/80. It seems like smart people contribute 20 percent of collective effort to something and get 80 percent of the rewards. You can follow this formula in your communication? Try to talk 20 percent of the time and listen 80. That is how you can learn to understand another person. You see, you cannot expect them to always come to the same ground with you especially when you are adamant in keeping to your own side. I am not asking you to agree with them gullibly, but meet them halfway by listening and reasoning. View things through their lens to understand where they are coming from. When people see that you are viewing things from their angle, they can become considerate of your opinion too.

And somehow, both parties can figure out common ground and find a resolution.

➤ LEARN THE CONTEXT

Efficient communication involves learning the context of the words. The same words can mean different things in different situations. It is the same with body language. So, whether spoken or written, it is important to understand the contexts of any communication. A worded fact is hard to understand if you do not know its context. So, do not rush with your conclusions until you have done your homework properly. Learn all the ins and outs. Then form your opinion or make a decision afterward.

➤ CREATE THE ATMOSPHERE

Communication is not only about talking or speaking. It is important to create a conducive environment for your communication. This is the only way to make your communication very effective. If you wish to understand another person and communicate your feelings or thoughts to them, then you need to create a welcoming and comfortable atmosphere for your communication.

➤ LEARN THE BODY LANGUAGE

It is good practice and advice learning the body language because it may help you put your own body under check during the process of communication. Plus, it helps you harness a deeper understanding of your company.

"The single biggest problem in communication is the illusion that it has taken place."

George Bernard Shaw

"The most important thing in communication is hearing what isn't said.

Peter Drucker

DECISION 5

DECISION TO
DELEGATE

5. DECISION TO DELEGATE

"Moses' father-in-law replied, 'What you are doing is not good. You and these people who come to you will only wear yourselves out. The work is too heavy for you; you cannot handle it alone." - Exodus 18:17-18

The decision to delegate is one of the best you can make as part of an effort to manage your own time. Learning to delegate frees up your time and allows you to attend to key priorities.

Delegating means handing over tasks and responsibilities to other people. You cannot do it all by yourself. The biggest problem with delegating is trust and control. Some people are obsessed with controlling everything in their lives or business. However, such total control limits you in your ability to grow. You have only certain time limits and certain capacities to manage things. Once you reach your limits, you'll stop growing if you fail to delegate things to others.

Delegation is therefore an art you should master. It's no good idea to be the first to trust others with your key priorities. So, start small if you do not have much experience with delegating.

Try delegating minor tasks first and then if everything goes well, proceed to larger tasks. Being able to delegate to the right people is another key element of success. You always have to match a person against a set task. If you trust small tasks to potent people, they get bored and frustrated. On the other hand, if you trust key tasks to people with no experience or with modest abilities, you get frustrated by them.

So, try to find a perfect match for your tasks. While it may be okay trusting people and delegating to them growth-stimulating tasks, the tasks should not be overwhelming. This is a wise way to delegate and avoid frustration.

Take time to communicate clearly your tasks to others and then take time to make sure they get you right. Miscommunication is one of the worst things that can happen in delegating. So, make sure you are on the same ground before delegating.

If you got used to controlling everything in your life, then delegating can be a tough thing for you to do. And it can be tough for those you delegate your tasks to if you start controlling them. Yes, of course, you need to stay informed on the progress, but you should not try to control the whole thing. This would only make people frustrated and angry - causing you to waste your precious time. The purpose of delegating is to save you time or free you up for other things. So, let go of tasks and delegate them to others. Let them get busy and get creative; let them grow and do their best in meeting your expectations.

> "Surround yourself with the best people you can find, delegate authority, and don't interfere as long as the policy you've decided upon is being carried out."
>
> **Ronald Reagan**

> "It's better to get ten men to do the work than to do the work of ten men!"
>
> **D.L. Moody**

DECISION TO HONOUR

6. DECISION TO HONOR

"The wise inherit honor, but fools get only shame." - Book of Proverbs 3:35

W e may or may not realize that there are certain things in life we owe others. Honor is one of them. Honor must be given to those who deserve it, who have earned it because of the great deeds they have done. We must also honor people for the position they occupy.

HONORING THOSE WHO DESERVE IT

First on the list of whom to honor are those through whom we came into this world, our parents. The Bible says, "Honor thy father and mother..." By extension, we must also honor our grandparents, uncles, and aunts. Our teachers, instructors, mentors, and others from whose knowledge and experience we have acquired lessons that guide our steps to greatness should make the honor list too.

Honoring deserving people is not an uphill task. If really their love, kindness, wisdom, and expertise have rubbed off on you, it shouldn't be hard to recognize them. However, some of us sometimes economize honour. We sometimes hesitate, because we are too shy, or not humble enough. Other times, we assume they know already that we have a lot of respect for them. But how so when we utter no words of acknowledgment to them. This is why you are being charged to decide. You must make honoring people a decision, not only in words but also in gestures expressed in action and attitude.

HONORING THOSE IN HONORABLE POSITIONS

This could be a more serious decision to make. Sometimes people in honorable positions do not match the call. God has ordained certain people in positions of honor, such as parents, in-laws, teachers, pastors, governors, etc. Unfortunately, sometimes these people's conducts are devoid of the characters that command honor. Some people struggle in life having fathers or mothers not worthy of honor. These people may not be kind or loving to you, which often hurts a lot. Nevertheless, honor us a must, at least for the sake of that position, if not for their sake.

It's a hard decision to make, but it can bring many blessings into your life.

WHY HONOR PEOPLE?

Apart from the fact that they deserve it and that they occupy certain positions, you do it for your own good.

Honoring people is something that tells of your personality. It shows the kind of person you are. It is a reflection of positive characters. If truly you are respectful, humble, and not vengeful, you will honor people regardless of things about things that seem not honorable. Honoring people is a noble habit. By your decision to honor, you are making it known to people the reputation you wish to have amongst them.

Apart from honoring people for the good of it, it also attracts rewards. Whatever you do, let it be known to you that there are people who are watching you. You do not know them or the fact that they are watching. You do not know where you would find yourself in the future where someone who has been watching you would be the one in the position to recommend you for something good. Even God is watching you. You know He is the ultimate rewarder. He promised us a long life if we honor our parents. That is just one of the numerous things He can do for us.

Therefore, make up your mind together to always honor people, starting from those around you to state leaders in your words and gestures.

"We value virtue but do not discuss it. The honest bookkeeper, the faithful wife, the earnest scholar get little of our attention compared to the embezzler, the tramp, the cheat."

John Steinbeck

"Honor is the presence of God in man."

Pat Conroy

DECISION TO
TAKE RISKS

7. DECISION TO TAKE RISKS

"Plans fail for lack of counsel, but with many advisers they succeed." - Proverbs 15:22

Here are two definitions for the word "risk" for you - "a situation involving exposure to danger" and "the possibility that something unpleasant or unwelcome will happen". Mostly, we deal with the second meaning of the word "risk" in our lives. It is something that at one time or the other in our lives, we would have a reason to do.

Making such a decision is never free of challenges. But there are things you can do to train yourself in making the right decisions - even when risk is obviously involved. Though these decisions potentially expose you to something "unpleasant or unwelcome", they are also capable of taking you out of your comfort zone.

You see, you can never hope to grow unless you step out of that comfort zone of yours. It's one of the most stimulating experiences we can have in our lives. However, risk-taking must be done with wisdom. Risk must be calculated. You should not jump into anything taking the risks just for the sake of it. Wise risk is all about planning and seeking proper, godly counsel.

When you make a decision to take a risk, you have to realize that the outcome may be unpleasant or unwelcome. You may lose full control of the situation when taking a risk as things may or may not turn out well. But be encouraged by the possibility of a desirable outcome. But that does not mean you have to be thoughtless in your decisions. Do all you can to attain the favourable outcome of your enterprise.

One person said, "Trust in God as if any success depended only upon Him, but do your part as if it all depended only upon you." See, these are the two sides of the same coin. Going ahead first and hoping for things to turn out all right is not wise. But trying to keep everything under your control restrains you to your own limitations. So, do your part and leave the rest to the Highest. But do your part well — plan things and seek advice from others. Only then can your risk pay back high dividends.

"Never was anything great achieved without danger."

Niccol Machiavelli

"A ship is safe in harbor, but that's not what ships are for."

William G.T. Shedd

DECISION TO SAY YES

8. DECISION TO SAY YES

"The heart of the righteous weighs its answers, but the mouth of the wicked gushes evil." - Proverbs 15:28

Saying "Yes" or "No" is the ultimate part of making decisions. Basically, all your decisions boil down to these simple words. Even for you picked up this book to read, it was preceded by a "Yes" to the title. If you are a man, you must have said, "Yes, I really want to be a man of value". You either say "Yes" or "No" to something or someone in your life. It's that simple. But bear in mind that saying yes just a part of a cycle of decision making.

Though a simple monosyllabic word, the emotions or thoughts behind it can be amazingly complicated. So much that if couched in words, a whole page of heart confessions can be penned; yet, you might only just be scratching the surface. Sometimes, emotional decisions are the best. For example, a family suddenly becomes homeless and you accommodate them in your little space knowing well that you have to give up your privacy. Compassion would not let you watch them languish on the streets. However, there are cases when they can lead you into serious problems. If your desperate quest for wealth just to silence your mocker leads you to say yes to an unbelievably profitable business without caring to analyze the processes involved or if it is even legitimate, to start with.

There are other times when the "yes" is motivated by reasoning alone. It can be a good thing to do if you make decisions on money, investment, business, etc. You want to first run a background check on the person or entity that introduced the business to you and ask questions from authorities such as a lawyer on the legal implications of the deal. So, learning to discern the motive behind your "yes" each time you want to say it is a good habit.

Still, reasoning cannot always serve the best for making the right decision. Sometimes, our minds tell us to say yes, while deep down in our hearts we strongly feel that we should say no. This is what we call intuition, which warns us against making wrong decisions.

What is the best way to say 'yes' in your life? It's learning to hearken to your emotions, your reasoning, and intuition all at once. The process is not easy. It takes lots of training to master. But after all, mastering your own self is one of the best things you can do in life. If you have control of your mind, your intuition, and your emotions, you'll get good chances of making the right choices in life.

Now "yes" is a powerful word. Once you say it to something or someone, you let them into your life. The yes decisions can be life-changing indeed. So, you need to be very careful as regards who or what you say "yes" to. You know, most people love those who easily say "yes". This means you can fall under some social pressure. Still, your "yes" is yours, you are the master of it. And there are times when you have to guard it and stand against some pressure to avoid letting wrong things come into your life.

> "Half of the troubles of this life can be traced to saying yes too quickly and not saying no soon enough."
>
> **Josh Billings**

> "Learn to say 'no' to the good so you can say 'yes' to the best."
>
> **John Maxwell**

DECISION TO SAY NO

9. DECISION TO SAY NO

"The heart of the righteous weighs its answers, but the mouth of the wicked gushes evil." - Proverbs 15:28

N o" is another powerful word. Mastering the art of saying "No" can save you lots of time and trouble. The problem with "No" is that most people do not like it. There are so many people or even businesses out there who wish you to say "yes" to them. Saying "yes" may mean spending your time, money, or efforts and sometimes these efforts do not bring you anything good in return, it probably only suits their selfish purposes.

But again, when you say "No", you become an unpopular person and you naturally experience a certain amount of pressure on you. Sometimes this pressure can be tough to bear. There are times when the pressure comes from strangers whom you do not really care much about. At other times the pressure against your "no" may come from the people you love. This in particular is the hardest to bear.

So, what are some of the tips that can help you to make a decision to say "No" and stick with it? One of such tips is to say no when you experience pressure to rush with your answer. Having no time to think things over oftentimes leads to making wrong decisions. This may be a sign of something sinister well hidden from you, only to surface in the course of time. So, if you are pressured to hurry up with your answer, it might be a safer thing to do to say "No", at least for the time being if not once and for all.

Another situation is when you have no peace about saying 'yes'. Your peace of heart and mind is a great criterion to take into account when making decisions. If something is bothering you inside, then say no or say later and take your time to think things over and discover what the problem is.

A good tip to follow in saying no to something is setting up your priorities. This may help you to avoid the hassle. If you know your priorities and you know what things come first, then it becomes easier to know if that thing makes your list or it is a distraction to discard.

Knowing your values also guides your decision to say no and stand your ground against pressure. If you know what is right, if you have certain values, then just stick with them - and say no to things that do not conform to those values. Sooner or later you would be rewarded for the right decisions. Plus, standing firm on your "no" may help you get rid of some unwanted people in your life. If these people do not share your values and morals, mounting pressure on you to betray your values, then why do you need them? You definitely do not.

"Misery loves company, but it hates confidence. Be bold enough to say NO to anyone who invites you to a pity party."

Unknown

"Self-respect is the root of discipline: The sense of dignity grows with the ability to say no to oneself."

Abraham Joshua Heschel

DECISION
TO READ

10. DECISION TO READ

"For gaining wisdom and instruction; for understanding words of insight." - Proverbs 1:2

It's a great pity today that the social media system is increasingly taking the place of reading in the minds of the younger generation. They'd rather watch TV or movies instead of reading. These things are not of equal worth. TV or movies can never replace books and reading. So, let's take a look at a few reasons to base your decision to read upon.

BOOKS CONTAIN WORDS

A major reason you need to read is that books contain words. You know that, of course. But do you remember that our world was created by the WORD? Words contain power. They have the power to change your mind and your soul. They have the power to redirect your life. Word is the most powerful thing you ever deal with in your life!

So, now you see that reading is a big responsibility. You need to make a decision to read, but you also are responsible for what you decide to read. Some books hold amazing and strong ideas. These ideas are like dynamite - they spark up the will in you to make great moves.

You know, reading is the next best thing to hear. Few of us have the privilege of being friends or acquaintance of great and wise people - we hear the words of their mouth from time to time. But those who don't have this privilege can at least get their books as virtually all of us can get the privilege to read their words and thoughts.

Picking books to read is similar to picking your friends. You would not want to associate with just anybody - let alone spend much time with unworthy people. The same rule applies to books. You have to be careful in selecting what books you decide to read. Spend time with the right books as books can either bring you up or tear you down.

THE NEED TO DEVELOP YOUR CREATIVITY

Now, this is another reason you need to read and you're probably not aware of it. Today's computer technologies allow directors to film such movies, which leaves little or no space for imagination. We may compare movies with mashed foods for babies and books with meat for adults. Often, movies provide you with information and stories well mashed. There is no need for chewing on them. They are ready to swallow.

The books are different. You have to process them, to "chew" on them. You have to use your imagination to make reading books interesting! Books make you grow faster - they develop you. Books allow you to share other people's experiences in life - to live through their stories. So, reading is an enriching experience.

> "You can never get a cup of tea large enough or a book long enough to suit me."
>
> **C.S. Lewis**

> "A reader lives a thousand lives before he dies, said Jojen. The man who never reads lives only one."
>
> **George R.R. Martin**

DECISION TO TELL THE TRUTH

11. DECISION TO TELL THE TRUTH

"Truthful lips endure forever, but a lying tongue lasts only a moment." - Proverbs 12:19

It's not an easy decision, to tell the truth. It's what I call a multi-layered decision. Have you noticed that making a decision, to tell the truth rarely works? You do mean to tell the truth. You are not a liar. You are a good person, but a time comes when you face the need, to tell the truth, or lie and… you twist it, just a little or you lie. Have you ever experienced such a thing before?

One of the reasons the decision, to tell the truth, is not easy because lie and fear go hand in hand. Many a time, we do not tell the truth because we are afraid of the consequences. Truth is not the most popular thing in our world. Telling the truth may lead to certain undesirable consequences. So, if you are set on making a decision, to tell the truth, you need to be ready to deal with your fear first.

Another "layer" of telling the truth decision is realizing the necessity. Sometimes, telling the truth evokes complications - to tell a lie can be so much easier. You forget to mention one little thing and you avoid undesirable complications and trouble. Who cares? It's just a trifle. But you know what? A lie is like cancer. It starts small, then grows bigger, and finally, it kills.

Telling the truth or lying is all about relationships. A thousand of small lies can kill your relationship the same way one big lie would. So, if you wish to decide to tell the truth, you need to realize how crucial it is. Telling the truth is not a matter of personal preference. It's a necessity in our individual lives - similar to breathing or eating. You cannot choose to breathe or not to breathe. Of course, you'll die if you dare stop breathing for more than five minutes. The same is applies to the case of telling the truth. If you start lying, sooner or later, you will kill yourself. Not literally though. But think about it: your integrity is an essence of your being; your reputation is your moral currency. When you lose these on account of lies, can you say you are still living?

Plus, telling lies builds up fear. You lie and you become afraid that people would discover those lies. Telling the truth frees you from such fears and allows you to be YOU - the real you. Truth sets you free from being counterfeit. You may object that sometimes the truth may hurt. That is so only if truth lacks the required level of love. Make a decision to speak the truth in love - for in love lies the strength of truth.

> "It is hard to believe that a man is telling the truth when you know that you would lie if you were in his place."
>
> **H. L. Mencken**

> "I can't say why people lie; they just do. Everyone has their own reasons for not telling the truth."
>
> **Eric Carr**

DECISION TO BE INSTEAD OF TO HAVE

12.DECISION TO BE INSTEAD OF TO HAVE

"Do not withhold good from those to whom it is due when it is in your power to act." - Proverbs 3:27

There is a great difference between having and being. We all dream to have a family, having a wife, having kids, having friends, having a good job, etc. This list can go on and on. The problem however is that only a few of us dream to be a husband, to be a father, to be a friend, etc. Having is fun and pleasant. It puts no responsibility on you.

Being is more challenging. You will take up tons of responsibilities upon yourself if you decide to be someone. Here is a simple example: You dream to have a wife and a family. You dream of all the happy times you'd have together. You get valid benefits from having a family. But how about dreaming of being a husband and a father?

What would you think about if you decide to be a husband? You take the responsibility of leadership over your family. You become their provider as well as their protector. You become the wall around your family guarding it against the troubles of this world. You become a decision-maker. It does not seem so fun anymore, right?

The difference between having and being is a big one. It's easy to make a decision to have, but it's much harder to make a decision to be. The decision to be can be made only by mature people. There is this universal law - you have to pay for everything you get. Responsibility is the payment for having. But responsibility also has high rewards to offer.

Once you get enough courage to be someone, then you enjoy the results of honor and achievement. God has put men in positions of power. However, those who do not make a decision to be and those who become dictators both fail to realize His plan. You cannot hope to be in the position of power unless you take up the responsibility for that position.

All the privileges granted by having a family, friends, or anything else in life can become rightfully yours only if you become the head of that family, the father, the friend, etc. You have to decide to be a friend, a husband, a father, a business person, etc. Make decisions and deal with the consequences of therefrom.

"Hold yourself responsible for a higher standard than anybody expects of you." Never excuse yourself.

Henry Ward Beecher

"You are responsible, forever, for what you have tamed."

Antoine de Saint-Exupery

DECISION TO BE FAITHFUL

13. DECISION TO BE FAITHFUL

**"for He guards the course of the just and protects the way of his faithful ones." -
Proverbs 2:8**

Faithfulness is the quality that reflects the character of God in your character. God is faithful - such is His nature. We, people, are bound to change, and making a decision to be faithful is not always easy. However, you can do it if you set your heart and mind on it.

You know, Jesus said that we should be faithful in small things first. Most of us have high aspirations in life - dreaming big dreams. Some of us hope for these dreams to come true right away. And we're frustrated if the immediate manifestation isn't forthcoming. Faithfulness is one of the key qualities you need to succeed. But none of us has it at the beginning. Faithfulness is the quality we have to grow and cultivate. So, starting small is essential. God, too, is always willing to entrust into your hands bigger things if He can find you faithful in small things.

It means faithfulness takes time to cultivate and test. It's a quality that is mostly tested time and troubles. So, how do you develop faithfulness? The root of this word is "faith". This means you have to believe in what you do while anchoring your faith in God alone. Those are the two key elements of faithfulness. A faithless person cannot be trusted with things.

Do you have a dream? Do you believe in that dream? How well do you believe in that dream? Do you believe enough to act upon your faith? Those are all vital questions to ask yourself. Faith is the starting point of faithfulness. If you undertake something, you get challenges on your way. Sometimes, faith is the only thing that motivates you to move on and not quit. And a faithful person is the one who does not quit halfway through. Such people are committed enough to go until the end.

Another aspect of making a decision to be faithful is having faith in God. There can be such circumstances in your life when you come to the limit of your strength and your self. That is the right time to trust in God. He can step in and help you make it through. So, besides natural commitment, a faithful person needs miracles and supernatural power in his or her life to remain faithful until the end.

"Your faithfulness makes you trustworthy to God."

Edwin Louis Cole

"Faithfulness and truth are the most sacred excellences and endowments of the human mind."

Marcus Tullius Cicero

DECISION TO BE HONEST

14. DECISION TO BE HONEST

"An honest answer is like a kiss on the lips." - Proverbs 24:26

The measure of your honesty is on par with your level of self-respect. Lying is disrespectful to others, but it's simply humiliating to you. You are the one who suffers the most from being dishonest. Honesty is also a foundation for relationships and dignity.

Now, making a decision, to be honest can sound foolish for some people. Some of us find lying expedient. It seems to make all the extra explanations unnecessary. It seems to make things simple and easy - at least for a while. That is the trickiest part. It's a lie that being dishonest makes things easier. Only the truth can set you free.

You see, once we get into a vicious circle of lying, it becomes hard to break out of it. And other people are not the only ones you cease to be honest with. Eventually, you start lying even to yourself. It is said that the bitter truth is better than the sweet lie. It's right because truth heals you while lies worsen your condition.

So, being honest is liberating. It heals you from inside out. A decision, to be honest, is also capable of healing your relationships. It is a habit you form. The same is true about saying lies. Once you form that nasty habit, it becomes hard to break out of it.

What do you do to carry out your decision, to be honest? First of all, start keeping a journal. Start by being honest with yourself. In all honesty, write down your thoughts - evaluating and judging your words or actions in your journal. It can be intimidating at first. But press on. It takes about 30 days of daily work to form a new habit. You'll start reaping the benefit once you form a habit of being honest with yourself.

You see, you open up your eyes and begin to see many problems when you decide to be honest with yourself. But equally, you begin to see many new opportunities. Plus, you get a chance to spot problems while they are still small and deal with them right away.

Your next step is to take the habit to a new level and dare to be honest with other people. Again, make it your goal to develop a habit of being honest. Stand against the temptation to lie and 'make things easier'.

The temptation to lie will come from time to time, consciously forming the habit of truth-telling builds you up in discipline, so you can break out of a lifestyle of falsehood.

"Honesty is the first chapter in the book of wisdom."

Thomas Jefferson

"It's discouraging to think how many people are shocked by honesty and how few by deceit."

Noel Coward

DECISION TO RECONCILE

15. DECISION TO RECONCILE

"All this is from God, who reconciled us to himself through Christ and gave us the ministry of reconciliation." - 2 Corinthians 5:18.

M aking a decision to reconcile with someone or something is good but it's not so easy. You know, this book is full of tough decisions to make. But they pave your way to excellence. Now, why is it so important to make a decision to reconcile? Who or what should we get reconciled to?

First of all, we should decide to reconcile with people in our lives. Such reconciliation has two sides to it. One is forgiving those who have done you harm and restoring relationships with them. The other one is reconciling with certain shortcomings in people. It means accepting people as they are.

Both of these aspects of reconciliation can benefit you greatly. For one, keeping old offenses and hard feelings in your heart rob you of new opportunities in life. The offenses may be minor, but the missed opportunities can be huge. So, make a decision to forgive, forget, and move on in your relationships.

The second aspect is getting reconciled with certain peculiarities or faults in other people and yourself. Some things are beyond your power - you cannot change them. You may find them irritating, annoying, or even exasperating. But what is the good of all this? You cannot change people or circumstances, but there is something you can change - your attitude towards them.

Your reaction to their actions is yours. You are responsible for it. You sure will get a more positive view of those people if you reconcile yourself with those peculiarities or shortcomings of theirs. And if you can do this, you are bound to notice a sudden change in them - they'll cease to drive you crazy and you'll start enjoying your life to the fullest.

Another part of the decision to reconcile is getting reconciled with your peculiarities and limitations. The world around us puts high pressure on people. They feel they have to perform well and become great achievers. That is why some people bite more than they can chew, so to say. An incontrovertible and wise decision is to know your strengths and gets reconciled with your weaknesses.

You'll want to open up your mind to overcome or work around your limitations if you know and get reconciled with those limitations. This very decision can be key to your success. Henry Ford is a good example of such decisions to reconcile. He had a dream of establishing a car company. He was a very literate man, but was not an engineer and knew very little of how to make cars.

He acknowledged his limitations and got reconciled with them. But he did not give up his dream. Being cognizant of his limitations, Ford focused on developing his strong sides rather than wasting time on his weaknesses. Those are his management skills - the ability to dream big and to stand up for his dream. The rest he has just outsourced to professionals.

This short story, hopefully, would help you make a decision to get reconciled with your limitations and turn them into a ladder to your success.

"The overall purpose of human communication is - or should be - reconciliation. It should ultimately serve to lower or remove the walls of misunderstanding which unduly separate us human beings, one from another."

M. Scott Peck, The Different Drum: Community Making and Peace

"The search for Jesus is about reconciling loss and tragedy to God and us."

W. Scott Lineberry

DECISION TO SET GOALS

16. DECISION TO SET GOALS

"Do not turn to the right or the left; keep your foot from evil." - Proverbs 4:27

Knowing how to set goals and pursue them saves you from living a drifting life. Others will do it for you if you do not set your own goals. That is how people get drifting through life; they become carried through life by the decisions and goals of other people.

Now, the science of setting goals is not rocket science. Goal setting isn't inborn with practically all humans. We, however, gain the ability in the course of life. So, let's take a look at some practical goal setting tips to help you make a decision to set goals.

› SET MEANINGFUL GOALS

You see, it is of no use setting goals unless they inspire you. Your goals have to be strong enough to motivate you into action - or else, they'll become burdens. So, if you do not know what goals to set, look for things that inspire you; look for something you love doing. It can become a source of ideas for goal setting.

› SET SMALL GOALS

Small goals are none the worse for their 'size'. You may read or hear people say that you need big goals to attain big things in life. That is true. But big goals have one problem- they can be very frustrating and daunting. You likely risk biting more than you can chew when venturing into big goals. So, if you are new to goal setting, start with smaller goals.

› SET FEASIBLE GOALS

Setting goals you cannot pursue and attain is meaningless. Your goals have to be doable. I mean, your goals have to be motivating enough to elicit a to-do list - which you'll follow very strictly. These goals have to be realistic and achievable.

SET SHORT-TERM AND LONG-TERM GOALS

A better way of planning your life such that you'll be making steady progress is by setting short-term and long-term goals. Some things are too big to fit into the frame of a single goal. This means you need to break them down into a range of smaller goals distanced in time. For example, you may plan your life for five years ahead. Some of the set goals would be attained only at the end of this period. But there certainly would be tons of smaller goals to pursue in the process. Those are the short-term goals.

As you may see, these are just a few practical tips that can help you to make a decision to set goals and teach you how to do it.

"Setting goals is the first step in turning the invisible into the visible."

Tony Robbins

"People are not lazy. They simply have impotent goals - that is, goals that do not inspire them."

Tony Robbins

DECISION TO FOLLOW

17. DECISION TO FOLLOW

"Now then, my sons, listen to me; do not turn aside from what I say." - Proverbs 5:7

The decision to follow requires wisdom. The following someone or something is a great way to learn and grow. Practical following in footsteps teaches you more than tons of books can. However, picking the wrong person to follow may lead to disastrous consequences.

Now, what does making a decision to follow demand? It requires a certain measure of obedience and submission. It means acknowledging someone's superiority over you and desires to learn from that person. All this may not sound very appealing in light of how our culture teaches us to become leaders and remain in charge of everything.

But the rule is that you cannot become a leader unless you learn how to follow. Even Jesus Christ had to come to this earth and follow others before it was His time to lead. It takes humility and deep self-respect. You have to understand that following a worthy person is not humiliating, but ennobling.

We all follow and lead at different times and areas of our lives. God is indisputably the best choice - if you have made up your mind to follow. He will lead you to excellence. However, following Him is not easy. His way is the way of love and sacrifice. It differs much from the ways of this world. Making a decision to follow God takes guts.

Now, picking your human leaders is a big decision to make, because you become shaped into the image of the one you are following. This decision should not be left to chances. It should not be forced on you by others. It has to be your own decision well fits your aspirations and convictions in life.

Keep in mind that when you follow a person, you learn their ways - whether good and bad. It's really hard to single out the good from bad in this situation. So, your decision to follow has to be well-grounded and you need to give much thought to it. One of the things to pay attention to when you pick a person to follow is their habits.

It is no new knowledge that picking up bad habits is easy. Habits and ideas are contagious. Getting rid of them can be hard. So, pay close attention to the habits of the person you intend to follow. There are many teachers, gurus, and coaches out there. They seem to carry great ideas and call people to follow them. But few of them are willing to let you see behind their bright ideas and great claims. Few of them let you into their personal lives.

Such teachers always evoke distrust. All you can see of them is what they tell you. They show you no action; they choose not to share any stories of challenges they dealt with within their lives. Overall, they seem to be way too perfect. When you make a decision to follow someone, you need to learn their real personality and then make a decision thereafter.

The end of life is to be like God, and the soul following God will be like Him.

Socrates

As far as things I avoid, I always avoid following trends just because they're trends.

Rachel Roy

DECISION TO LEAD

18. DECISION TO LEAD

"The path of life leads upward for the prudent to keep them from going down to the realm of the dead." - Proverbs 15:24

A great way to find out if you are a leader is to turn around and see if anyone is following you. This is true to a high degree. Some people pride themselves on leadership - believing they're good leaders - while no one is actually interested in following them!

Let's take a look at some of the tips on making a decision to lead.

> IF YOU WANT TO LEAD, YOU NEED TO LEARN TO FOLLOW FIRST

No one is born a leader. We all learn to master this art. You learn leadership through the following. The key idea here is to pick the right person to follow after. If you want to be a respectable leader, pick and follow a strong leader - get mentored by them.

> CONSTANT GROWTH

Leaders cannot stop - sitting idly by. If you want to be a leader, you need to make a decision to grow. You are the one responsible for your personal growth. It all depends on you and it's your sole responsibility. The rest of it is just making excuses.

> VISION

Without vision, you are bound to become a blind leader. It is a vision that announces a leader amidst a crowd - singling them out of the crowd.

➤ GOALS

A good leader must be very proficient when it comes to goal setting. Once you gain vision, you need to be able to break it down into a set of achievable goals and lead people into pursuing them.

➤ MOTIVATION

You cannot hope to be a leader without a strong self-motivation. You have to know how to motivate your own self to action along with others. Leaders have to be inspirational; they need to possess the skills to motivate others.

➤ PEOPLE SKILLS

Leadership is all about communicating with people. Developing strong people skills is one of the things you need to do if you're making a decision to lead.

➤ TEAM SKILLS

A leader needs to be able to organize single people into teams. A great team can do wonders in terms of pursuing goals and fulfilling vision. But teaming up people can be left to a chance. That is what leaders are for.

➤ RESPONSIBILITY

Leadership is all about responsibilities and willingness to deal with the consequences of your decisions. Excuse making is unbecoming of a good leader. Owning up mistakes does not undermine your leadership position. It gives you more opportunities to fix them and grow.

"Effective leadership is not about making speeches or being liked; leadership is defined by results, not attributes."

Peter Drucker

"Don't find fault, find a remedy."

Henry Ford

DECISION TO LEAVE

19. DECISION TO LEAVE

"Leave your simple ways and you will live; walk in the way of insight." - Proverbs 9:6

Making a decision to leave becomes inevitable sometimes in life. It can be a painful decision because our past becomes a part of us. Still, the decision to leave can be a life refreshing decision. Let's take a look at when or why such a decision should be made.

➤ DECISION TO LEAVE A JOB

There can be several reasons to leave a job. For one, you may have simply outgrown that position of yours — and you are not being promoted by virtue of the experience garnered on the job. If you want to grow and move on with your life to the next level, you may have to leave that office. This decision has an inherent excitement element because you are moving on to new prospects.

But you may also deal with fear, as new things too can have an element of uncertainty about them.

➤ DECISION TO LEAVE HOME

This decision to leave has to be made when it is due. We all have to grow and become independent. That is the time for us to leave our home and find a new space for living. Some parents are so in love with their children that they make their decision to leave a tough one. They may make your life so comfortable - that you may not want to move on. Still, this decision has to be made.

➤ DECISION TO LEAVE YOUR FRIENDS

There are times when we have to make a decision to leave our friends. When you receive the Lord, your values change. Hopefully, your style of life changes, too. There are things you used to do in the world and you enjoyed doing them with your friends. But when you become a believer, your point of view on those things change.

Not all your friends would be favorably disposed to such changes. Some of them may try to pull you down into the same old ways and sins you used to love. If they cannot understand you and you cannot compromise your values, then it is certainly time to leave them behind.

The decision to leave automatically introduces changes into your life. These changes can be positive or negative, but if you trust your life to God, you can cope with them.

"All changes are more or less tinged with melancholy, for what" we are leaving behind is part of ourselves."

Amelia Barr

"It's very easy to say no to leaving the house."

William Shatner

DECISION TO
BE FOCUSED

20. DECISION TO BE FOCUSED

"Let your eyes look straight ahead; fix your gaze directly before you." - Proverbs 4:25

Staying focused is one of the key abilities you need to attain your dreams and be successful. Perpetual distraction leaves you with little or no headway towards your dream. So, let's take a look at some tips on making a decision to stay focused.

KNOW YOUR GOALS AND STAY FOCUSED

Once you set your goals, keep on thinking about them. Draw plans and follow through. Take a few moments during the day to verbalize your goals. Hearing those goals helps you to stay focused on them.

WRITE THINGS DOWN

When you make a decision to stay focused, it's hard to keep everything in your head. Your main thoughts should be dedicated and should stay focused on your main goals. So, write down all the minor tasks and in-between goals you pursue. This would help you free up your mind from other things and get focused on your key goals.

SET DEADLINES

If you make a decision to be focused on your goals or something else in your life, you should set deadlines. Indefinite projects never get accomplished. With milestones and deadlines attached, break down larger goals into smaller sets.

MAKE ROOM

If you have decided to be focused on something very important, you should make room for it. For instance, if you have decided to be focused on your family, you need to make room for it. Building up relationships or growing your kids takes time. So, plan It and make time for it. Free up your time by cutting out some of the other activities and goals. You have to sacrifice things if you decide to be focused on something.

Do not set too many goals to stay focused on. You cannot do it all. So, you have to prioritize your goals and stay focused on the most important ones.

TAKE BREAKS

Staying focused on something all the time is hard. You get tired easily and burn out. If you wish to have enough motivation to keep you through the time, you need to take breaks and get some fun. When you change your activities and thoughts for a short while, you get back to your goals and become even more able to stay focused on them.

"Stay focused on the mission."

Naveen Jain

"Stay focused, go after your dreams, and keep moving toward your goals."

LL Cool J

DECISION TO LIVE RIGHT

21. DECISION TO LIVE RIGHT

"The Lord's curse is on the house of the wicked, but he blesses the home of the righteous." - Proverbs 3:33

Living right has many great benefits. However, it also comes with a great number of challenges. Integrity is a great intangible asset you can accumulate. However, as it is with any asset, integrity takes investment. So, let us take a look at a few things you need to know when making a decision to live right.

IT BEGINS WITH ATTITUDE

You act upon what you believe to be right. So, if you decide to live right, first learn to think and feel right. Jesus said that all the words and actions come out of the abundance of heart. Thus, true integrity is an issue of the hearth.

TAME YOUR EMOTIONS

If you want to live right and be true in your words and actions, you need to tame your emotions and thoughts first. How can this be done? It can be done by implementing self-discipline and by setting up boundaries for yourself.

Every person should have the inner boundaries. There is a point of thought and emotion, where you say, "No, it's enough!" You cannot say so to others unless you say so to yourself first. You see, integrity gives you authority. If you hold on to your values and do not compromise them, then you can teach others. We are not talking of judgment here. If you make a decision to live right, it does not give you the right to judge other people. But, it gives you the authority to teach them.

SET STANDARDS

To live right, you have to have some sort of standard to match all your thoughts, words, or deeds against. His Words are that standard for you if you believe in God. Of course, none of us is perfect and none of us can keep the law perfectly. Only by the grace of God we live. But that does not mean we should merely exist and not strife for the utmost.

When you make a decision to live right, you have to be prepared for some measure of failure. We all make mistakes. They are the inevitable part of life. So, having had the confidence of setting your heart on the best, do not judge or condemn yourself if you fail to attain it. Keep on striving instead. Setting a high goal and attaining half of what has been set is much better than not setting any goal at all!

"If you ain't loving life, you ain't living right."

Unknown

"I never had a policy; I have just tried to do my very best each and every day."

Abraham Lincoln

DECISION TO PIONEER SOMETHING

22. DECISION TO PIONEER SOMETHING

"All who are prudent act with knowledge, but fools expose their folly." - Proverbs 13:16

At times we all feel that life gets somewhat stale. We lose vigor and motivation. We fail to enjoy it as much as we used or ought to. What does it mean? It may mean a time for a change has come. Making a decision to pioneer something is always a great idea. Willingly, you choose to walk on a new path. You know, scientists have discovered that people are afraid of unknown much more than they are afraid of known bad outcomes.

So, it takes courage to tread a new path and to become a pioneer. However, there are times and situations in our lives when the only real solution is to try something new. The old and beaten ways seem to fail us entirely. They cease to be satisfactory. That may be a time to decide and pioneer something.

Another reason to become a pioneer is when you need to avoid competition. This is true in business. Old ways and old niches may have a tough competition in them. Thus, pioneering something new opens up a way to a competition-free realm. There is one person who has become a life coach and on-line guru, sharing his insights with people.

This niche of business is filled with competitions. Trying to rank high as a coach and trying to stand out of the crowd of other life coaches may become boring and tiring. So, what did he do in his case? He pioneered something. He stopped trying to position and promote himself as a life coach. Instead, he chose his name as a brand. He started to market his own name as his brand - an expression of what he does or has to offer and succeeded in that endeavor. You know what? If you type in "life coach" into Google, you get hundreds of pages. But if you type in someone's name, you get just one or few there.

So, he pioneered this approach and placed himself completely above all competition. That is a great way to do something new. However, you have to believe strongly in whatever pioneering decision you make. It would never work for you if you do not enjoy or believe in it.

Thus, faith and courage are two of the cornerstones of making a decision to pioneer an idea. And, you certainly need wisdom and planning to make you succeed in your undertaking.

"Insanity: doing the same thing over and over again and expecting different results."

Albert Einstein

"A mistake is simply another way of doing things."

Katharine Graham

DECISION TO SUCCEED

23. DECISION TO SUCCEED

"He holds success in store for the upright, he is a shield to those whose walk is blameless." - Proverbs 2:7

We all want to be successful. But the biggest trouble with success is the benchmark with which we measure it. You see, the world has its own benchmark to measure you with. If you fail to meet the standard, they label you as a failure. God has a very different approach to measuring success. He views people differently than we do.

So, one of the first things to do as you make a decision to succeed is to find the right benchmark with which you will measure your success. Picking the wrong standard can get you easily frustrated in all of your attempts. Or, you can be headed in the wrong direction. And you'll find it highly unsatisfactory once you attain what you thought to be a success.

The next step is developing a strong self-motivation. If you are unable to motivate yourself to act in a field of your choice, there is no way you can succeed in it. You need to plan your activities and set your objectives, but you also have to get proactive and motivate yourself to act upon your plans.

Another key element of success is following successful people. Once you clearly define what success means to you, go ahead and find successful people in the area. Today, it's easy to do this by reading their blogs or books. You see, one of the easiest ways to succeed is to find something that works and "copy it". Try to understand how those successful people manage to succeed. What habits do they have that you do not have? What decisions have they made? How active are they?

You can pioneer your own way to it once you can learn the ways of others to their success. Copying those laudable things others have done. But pioneering new things is even better. You are a unique person with unique talents from God. You can overcome all the obstacles on your way to success —you only need to believe in Him and yourself.

Now, fear is one of such obstacles. There are millions of people out there who fail way before they even start. The fear of failure holds them back from pursuing their goals and they fail right then and there. That is the worst kind of failure indeed. You may try something, fail at it, but still, you gain useful experience and you learn. But when you let the fear hold you back, you fail with no merit gained. The fear can be overcome by faith. Faith is the best motivator ever. So, build up your faith and pave your way to success.

"In order to succeed, your desire for success should be greater than your fear of failure."

Bill Cosby

"A successful man is one who can lay a firm foundation with the bricks others have thrown at him."

David Brinkley

DECISION TO
BE CONFIDENT

24. DECISION TO BE CONFIDENT

"From the fruit of their lips people are filled with good things, and the work of their hands brings them reward." - Proverbs 12:14

Self-confidence should never be confused with arrogance. There is a difference between arrogance and confidence. An arrogant person goes on about what he is worth in order to make impressions. A confident person on the other hand does not blow his own trumpet, neither does he silence it. Whenever and wherever he appears, his virtue just shines through on its own without him pushing it. If you are sure you have value to offer to your world, you should never let yourself be intimidated. To build your confidence, here are some tips to help you:

> UNDERSTAND THAT NO ONE IS PERFECT

Many people feel inferior to others because they feel so imperfect. No one is perfect. Even the most confident people make mistakes and fail. You see, those people are confident despite their faults. This means, you too can be.

> LEARN TO LOOK PEOPLE IN THE EYE

If you feel uncomfortable and lack confidence, it's hard for you to look people in the eye. Start forming a new confidence habit from this day on. Give yourself the challenge to try and look at least 10 people in the eye every day.

> BELIEVE IN YOURSELF

God has created you after His own image and likeness. This means you are a worthy person. Even if you have made some mistakes and sins in your life, God is willing to forgive you and forget your past. So, why should you keep on thinking of those mistakes? Why should you allow those mistakes to destroy your self-respect and faith in yourself? Nothing is possible without faith. If you lack self-belief, then how do you expect others to do so?

It's time to ask for God's forgiveness of your past; it's time to forgive yourself and move on with confidence.

› THINK AND SPEAK GOOD THINGS ABOUT YOURSELF

You know it's not good to say bad things about others. But sometimes we forget that it is equally bad to say negative things about ourselves. Some people get in the habit of saying negative things or criticizing themselves. This speech may go on just in your mind. Or, you may speak out loud.

If you make a decision to build up your confidence, you need to learn to think and say good and positive things about yourself.

› WATCH YOUR BODY LANGUAGE

We speak not only with our lips, but our bodies, too. Body language gives out a confident or shy person. Start analyzing your behavior. Take time to examine the way you speak and the way you hold yourself in a mirror. Train yourself to behave the right way. This would boost your inner confidence.

> "Believe in yourself! Have faith in your abilities! Without a humble but reasonable confidence in your own powers you cannot be successful or happy."
>
> **Norman Vincent Peale**

> "Optimism is the faith that leads to achievement. Nothing can be done without hope and confidence."
>
> **Helen Keller**

DECISION
TO DREAM

25. DECISION TO DREAM

"The prospect of the righteous is joy, but the hopes of the wicked come to nothing." - Proverbs 10:28

We all have dreams. Even small kids dream of things. Often, these dreams reflect our inner drives. They show us the things we enjoy the most in our lives. Dreams reveal our inner inclinations and talents. It's only natural that people who are courageous enough to pursue their dreams are happier than those who refuse to give their dreams a chance.

Dreaming has a certain power in it. For one, dreams are highly inspirational and motivational. There are millions of people who merely exist just because they lack motivation. If you can dream big and fall in love with your dream, you'll find a great source of motivation.

Dreams have the power to drive us through life. If we refuse to follow the dreams willingly, they may move us to certain actions subconsciously. There is a danger in such doing. If you let your dream to drive you subconsciously through life, you may end in a nightmare.

You see, dreams lead you to dream life only if you make the conscious choice of making them come true. Dreams can come true if you know how to turn them into goals and pursue those goals.

Having dreams as your advisers is not always the best way to live. Dreams do not have the intellect to make the right decisions and to pave the way to success. But you do. So, the trick is to be inspired and motivated by your dreams but to make all your decisions consciously.

How do you turn your dreams into goals? You need to make them practical and doable. It is not an easy task though. That is why you should test run your dreams first. Focus on something you dream about. Try to imagine that this thing has come true. How do you feel about it? Is the effort worth it at all? Are you willing to put much work into making this dream come true? Take your time and single out the dearest dreams of your life. And then consciously turn them into the driving force and motivation source of your life.

"All human beings are also dreaming beings. Dreaming ties all mankind together."

Jack Kerouac

"Man is a genius when he is dreaming."

Akira Kurosawa

DECISION TO
BE POSITIVE

26. DECISION TO BE POSITIVE

"A happy heart makes the face cheerful, but heartache crushes the spirit." - Proverbs 15:13

Positive thinking gives you an advantage. If you stay positively tuned, your mind and body give a more adequate reaction to situations. You'll remain calm and avoid being excessively stressed out. Optimism helps you turn your challenges into opportunities. So, let's take a look at some tips on how to make and carry through the decision to be positive.

> BE GRATEFUL

Gratefulness fixes your thoughts on positive and good things around you. It seems like everything in our world has two sides to it - a good one and a bad one. Gratefulness helps us to see the good one. When we recall all the good things we can say thank you for, we cast away the gloomy thoughts.

> BE REALISTIC

Some people say that optimistic people are foolish because they do not have a realistic view of things. That is not true. In this case, pessimists cannot be considered realists, too. When you get focused on bad things, they tend to grow in size in your mind. Then even a small white weft may turn into a menacing thunder cloud.

Staying positive becomes much easier when you gain a more realistic view of things. Usually, things are not as bad as we tend to view them.

> HELP OTHERS

Helping others may keep you positively tuned. If you do something and you become active seeing the results of your activity. In most cases, you get people's gratitude, too. All this keeps you positively tuned in your mind and heart.

➤ CHANGE YOUR THINKING PATTERNS

A decision to be positive is not one that can be carried out fast or easily. If your mind has gotten into the negative pattern of thinking, then you have to break it out of it. Start by taking 15 mins every day to think of something good. Pray and thank God for His blessings. No petitions, just gratitude.

➤ GET NOURISHED WITH POSITIVE INFORMATION

Read good books, listen to good music, get inspired, talk to cheerful people, cut down the news time, read the Bible, pray, watch good movies, etc. Too often our minds get fed up with negative information - leading to forming negative thoughts. Cut out that source and provide your mind with a solid diet of positive thoughts and impressions.

Hopefully, these simple tips would lay the foundation for your decision to be positive and to succeed in life.

"Life is hard. It gets even harder when you think it is really hard, and gets easier when you set your mind positive."

Unknown

"Pessimism leads to weakness, optimism to power."

William James

DECISION TO WALK WITH GOD

27. DECISION TO WALK WITH GOD

"Thus you will walk in the ways of the good and keep to the paths of the righteous." -
Proverbs 2:20

Walking with God is the best decision to make in life. It's different from a decision to believe in God. Walking involves more than mere church attendance, Bible reading, or praying. Jesus once asked a question - how can two people walk together if they do not agree? They can't. So, walking with God means living in agreement with Him - you head in the same direction and you aim for the same destination.

So, how do you practically go about the decision to walk with God? Below are some points to guide you:

› LEARN WHERE GOD GOES

You cannot make a decision to walk with God and go your way. God won't change His direction for yours. You are the one who should tune-up to His plans. So, first, learn where God is headed. Some things are easy to learn. You read the Bible and you discover what is right and what is wrong. Then you refuse to do what is wrong and do what is right.

However, a true walk with God requires a more intimate relationship with Him and a deeper knowledge of His thoughts and His heart.

› LEARN TO HEAR GOD

Born again Christians can and should learn to hear God's voice. He has provided general "logos" directions in His word. But He has also personal "Rhema" directions to give for your life. He has mapped a course for you and you can learn it and follow it by walking with God. To hear God, you must create around yourself a spiritual environment. This requires that you keep away or eliminate sights and sounds of things of the flesh. These include what you read, what you watch on TV, the music and messages you listen to. Replace these with spiritual ones. This is what helps you be in the spirit. And you only hear God when you are in the Spirit.

> GET ACTIVE

Once you find the direction, start walking. Stop hesitating and get to the action. I know, sometimes doing what is right may be tough. You may deal with various challenges on the way - you may face opposition. But all those things are nothing to God. Yes, they may look big to you, but what are they to Him? Nothing! You are bound to overcome all the obstacles on the way if you walk with God in your life.

> COMMUNICATE

There are times when we lose our connection with God. These are the times when we make mistakes and stray away from His course. Always get reconnected with God. He'll wait for you and He'll pick you up and walk on with you. You see, He has never expected you to be flawless. He knows we are dust, so He tunes His step to us - as parents tune their step to their babies.

Walking with God may be the hardest thing you do in your life, but it is the most satisfying one, too.

"Those who walk with God, always reach their destination."

Henry Ford

"To walk with God is to walk in the light of God's countenance; to live as people who remember that all things are naked and opened unto the eyes of Him with whom we walk."

J.C. Ryle

DECISION TO
BE DIFFERENT

28. DECISION TO BE DIFFERENT

"The fear of the LORD leads to life; then one rests content, untouched by trouble." - Proverbs 19:23

We all are different. God made us that way. However, our culture insists on forming us and shaping us into the same image and likeness of this world. And such conformation is a serious issue. Sometimes, it even costs people their lives. It usually starts at an early age. Teens first try cigarettes, and then they try alcohol. They may end up being addicts.

The whole thing starts with the fear of being different. So, the decision to be different is a crucial one. You need to know what is right and stand up for it. Being different means you own your values by sticking to them. Being different also means the freedom to be you. God has created you to be a unique person with unique talents and perceptions. If you have the fear of God, i.e. you agree with His standard on what is good and what is evil and follow them; you get the freedom to be you.

Some people say that faith in God limits your freedom. In reality, our modern culture limits people much more. It dictates to you how you should dress and what you should look like. It dictates what you should think and how you should behave - enforcing its standards on what is success and what is a failure. It measures you constantly with a ruler and punishes you for not being able to meet its standards.

So, the decision to be different liberates you from this bondage. Since God has created you, He knows who you are and what you are like. Thus His commandments cannot possibly limit or cage your personality. Meeting His standard brings the better you out. You get the freedom to become the best without having to compare yourself with other people.

You see, there is no need to match yourself against His other creations since God has made you unique. A unique person deserves a unique standard to be matched against. It has nothing to do with our mass culture wherein everyone is matched against the same benchmark. So, make a decision to be different not just for the sake of standing out of the crowd. Make a decision to be different for the sake of reaching your utmost potential and fulfilling your goal in life.

> "I'm not different for the sake of being different, only for the desperate sake of being myself. I can't join your gang: you'd think I was a phony and I'd know it."

Vivian Stanshall

DECISION TO
BE RESPONSIBLE

29. DECISION TO BE RESPONSIBLE

"Do not love sleep or you will grow poor; stay awake and you will have food to spare." - Proverbs 20:13

Being responsible is a sign of maturity. You cannot take up responsibility for others until you learn to be responsible for your own self. A responsible person is someone who has just a few excuses to offer. So, let's take a look at some tips on how to make and carry out a decision to be responsible.

➤ BE OBEDIENT

There are many situations in our lives, when we have to be obedient. These situations occur in our families, at work, or on the social level. You know, being obedient is your responsibility in virtually all situations. And you need to know how to carry it out. The problems start when we neglect this responsibility. That is how some people get in trouble with the law. They just fail to be responsible for their obedience.

➤ CONFRONT PROBLEMS

Responsible people do not wait for others to come and solve their problems. They make the first step to confronting problems. The good thing about it is that if you confront your problems, you do not give them a chance to grow big. It may not be a pleasant thing to do, but the word 'responsibility' does not mean 'pleasure'. It is something that has to be done no matter what.

➤ ANSWER FOR YOUR WORDS AND ACTIONS

Do not blame anyone else for what you do. Do not come up with excuses for your words or actions. Be answerable for them. This involves making another decision - the decision to have courage. You need to be able to own up to your mistakes.

Only in this case would you be able to fully own up your successes. If you say, 'bad luck' in the case of failure, then people would say "he got lucky", when you attain success.

➤ TAKE INITIATIVE

If you make a decision to be responsible, then you do not have to be pushed to anything. You should take the initiative. Some people wait for their family members to push them into some decisions. They can never make up their minds about anything. This a far cry from a life of responsibility.

➤ TAKE A STAND

If you want to be a responsible person, then you need to take a stand for your decisions. You make them, you stand up for them and you bear the guilt or praise for the outcomes.

"Freedom makes a huge requirement of every human being. With freedom comes responsibility. For the person who is unwilling to grow up, the person who does not want to carry is own weight, this is a frightening prospect."

Eleanor Roosevelt

"Accept responsibility for your life. Know that it is you who will get you where you want to go, no one else."

Les Brown

DECISION TO HAVE COURAGE

30. DECISION TO HAVE COURAGE

"The wicked flee though no one pursues, but the righteous are as bold as a lion." - Proverbs 28:1

C ourage is not something we get born with. It is a quality that we develop as we deal with various circumstances.

Courage has two aspects - a moral and a physical one. It is a certain reaction provided by your body and by your soul. You can train your body to react properly in certain circumstances. And the same can be done with your soul. Now, moral courage is your ability to do what is right regardless of what other people may say or think about you. In our days when opinions of others seem to be so important, making a decision to have courage used to be a tough one. Still, being courageous makes you more independent and mature in your thoughts, words, and actions.

The word "courage" derives from the word "cor" or heart. This means the root of your courage is in your heart. How do you carry out your decision to have courage? By watching your heart and by investing good things into it.

BE HONEST WITH YOURSELF.

That takes courage. Honestly analyzing your thoughts, desires and behavior take guts. Then move on to saying the truth. Say what you believe in. Say what you think. This does not suggest that you utter unbridled speech. But train yourself to be courageous by saying the truth, when you have a chance to lie.

START SOMETHING NEW

Become a pioneer. Discover new ways of doing things. Or, just try to break out of the beaten path of your life. Get the courage to make changes for good. You may start with your family. Take the initiative and bring about positive changes.

RENDER HELP AND STAND UP FOR PEOPLE.

This is another step to carry out your decision to have courage. Look for people who need your help and become the first one to offer it. Do not wait for being asked for it. If you see someone who is in trouble, stand up for them. Stand up for your family, for your kids. Stand up for your church and for what you believe to be true. Courage takes both inner work and actions to manifest it.

"All our dreams can come true if we have the courage to pursue them."

Walt Disney

"Success is not final, failure is not fatal: it is the courage to continue that counts."

Winston Churchill

DECISION TO BECOME A PRODUCER

31. DECISION TO BECOME A PRODUCER

"One person gives freely, yet gains even more; another withholds unduly, but comes to poverty." - Proverbs 11:24

A producer is one who comes up with a product to meet people's needs at a price. He is the opposite of a consumer. Our modern culture strives to turn all of us into consumers. We consume ready-made things: information, concepts, technologies, and many more, but we rarely create them. We may take part in the process, but only a few of us retain the privilege of creating something from start to end.

We've been trained to consume. However, a mature man cannot be characterized only as a consumer. A real man has to deliver value to other people. He has to know how to use the consumed good for creating something new and great. If you look at examples of all the great men remembered by history, you'd see them as great producers. History never remembers great consumers

In ancient times, people lived differently. They were more independent. Many people used to be farmers or crafters. They did not depend so much on others for survival. They knew how to produce good products; they knew how to create value. That is one reason till this day we pay a lot of money for antiques.

We live in the days of disposable things. We consume them and we throw them away. The disposable mentality has greatly affected us both in growth and relationships. If other people fail to satisfy our desire to consume, we easily throw them away. It's time for you to sit down and calculate your consumption to production ratio.

How much value do you produce for your family? There are millions of men out there who want to be waited on by their wives and kids. They do not deliver any value to their families. How much value do you produce for your company or business? How much value do you produce for your country? If you are willing to make a decision to be a producer, you need to ask yourself all those questions and get honest answers.

"Every man is a consumer and ought to be a producer."

Ralph Waldo Emerson

"Work to survive, survive by consuming, survive to consume: the hellish cycle is complete."

Raoul Vaneigem

OTHER BOOKS BY
ABRAHAM GREAT

∙

31 Decisions that make a man of value

Understanding Values

Reconnecting Disconnected Generations

iThrive

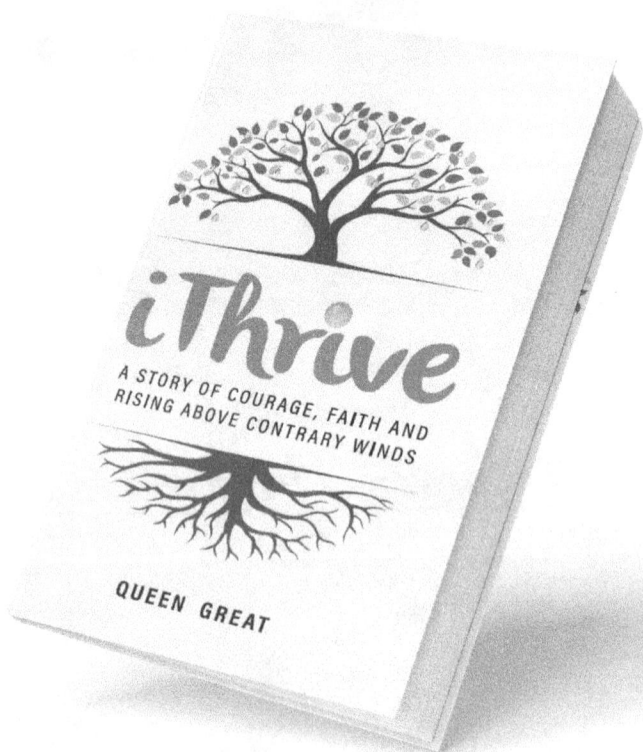